Tim Did It

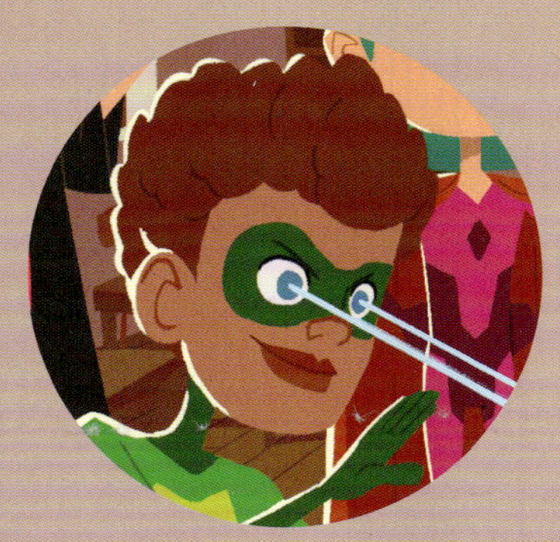

Written by
Daisy Hawkins

Illustrated by
Nicolas Rix

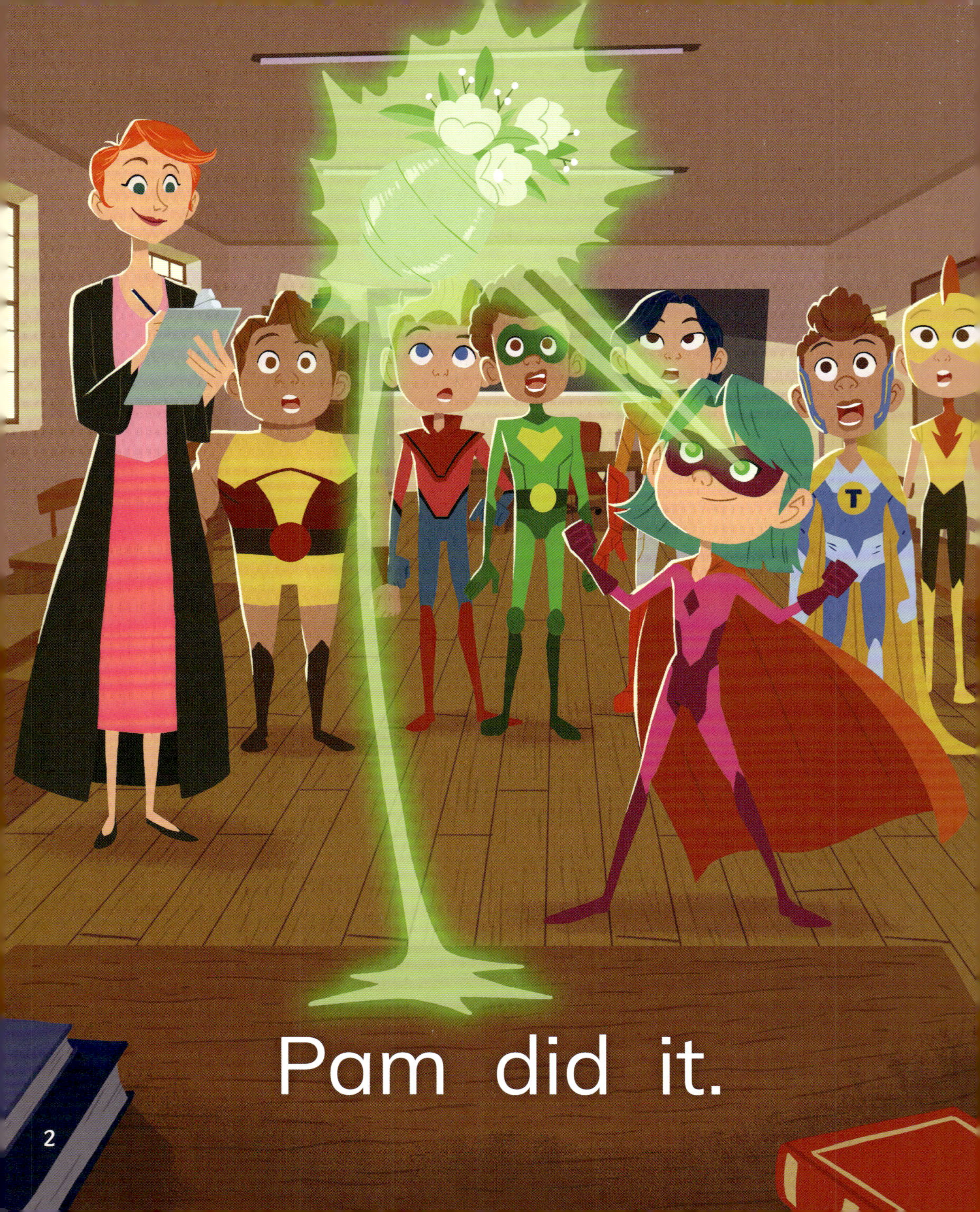

Pam did it.

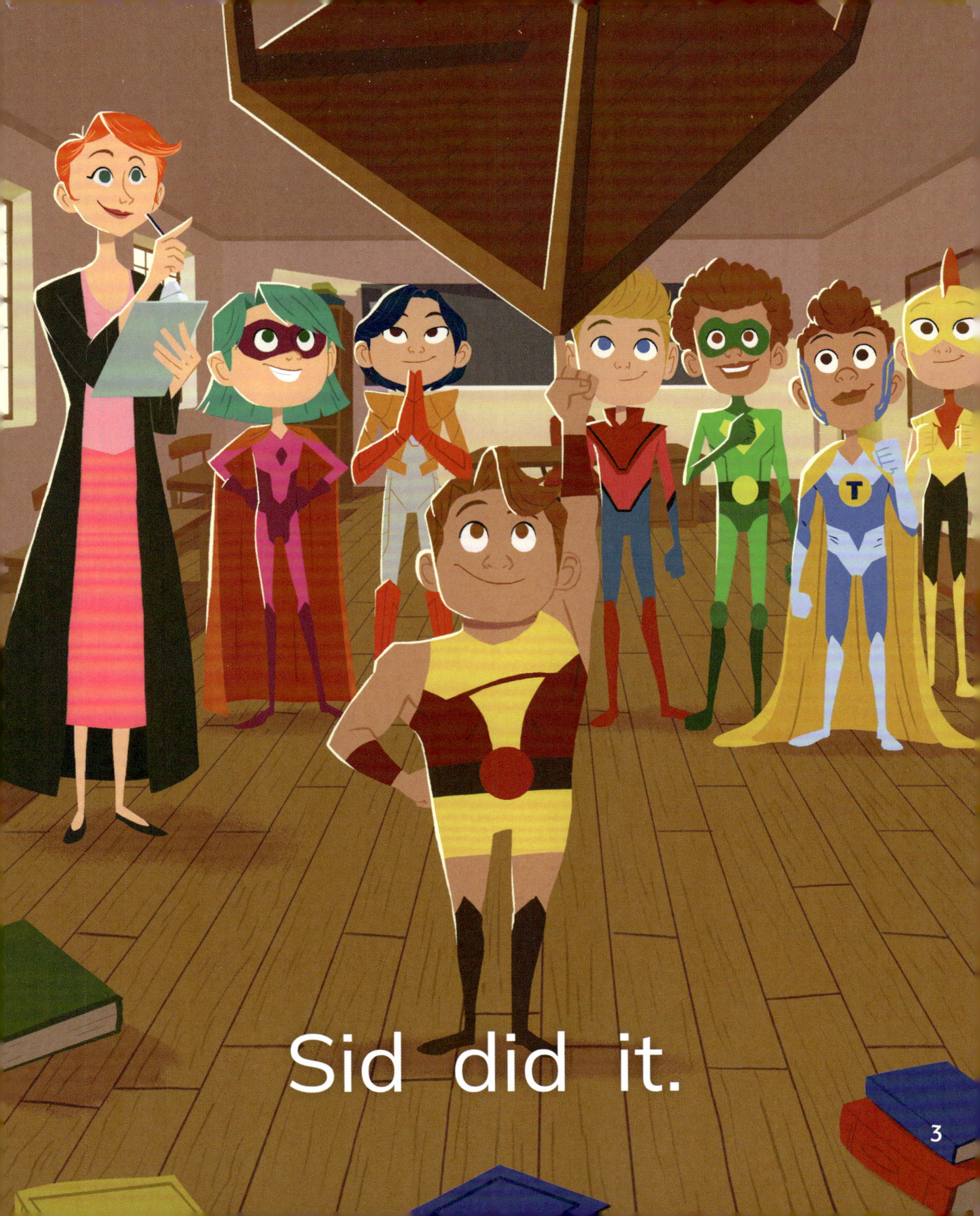

Sid did it.

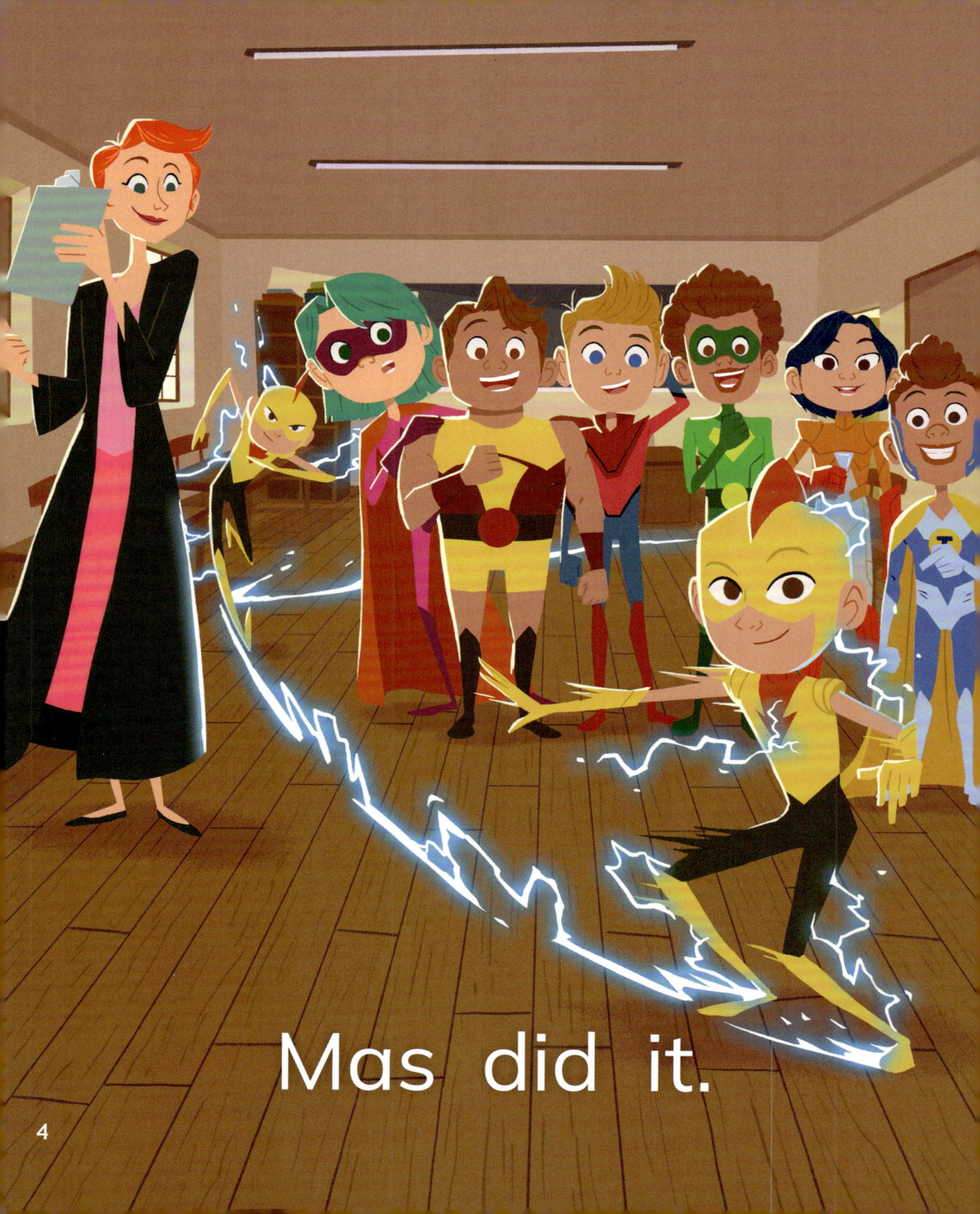

Mas did it.

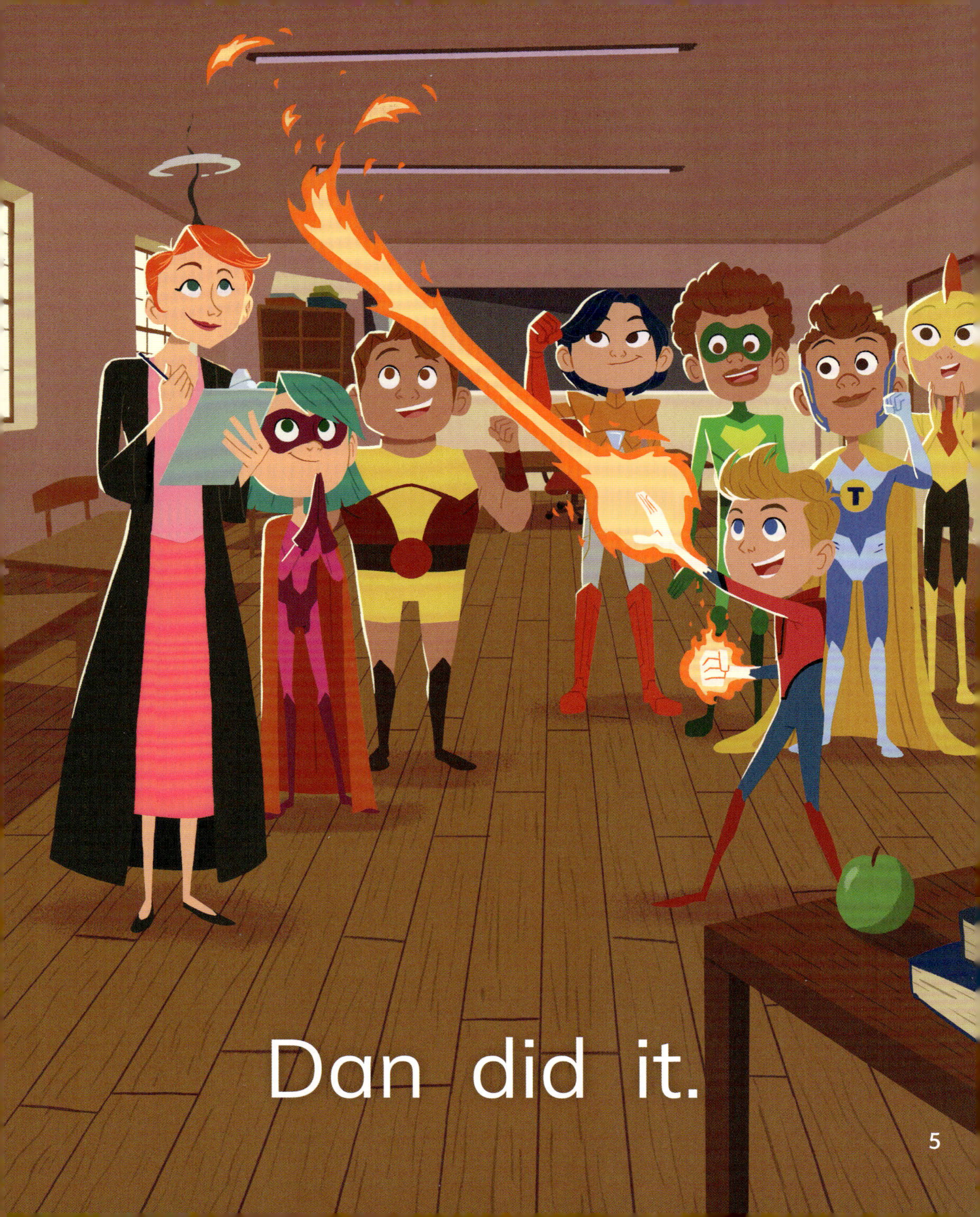

Dan did it.

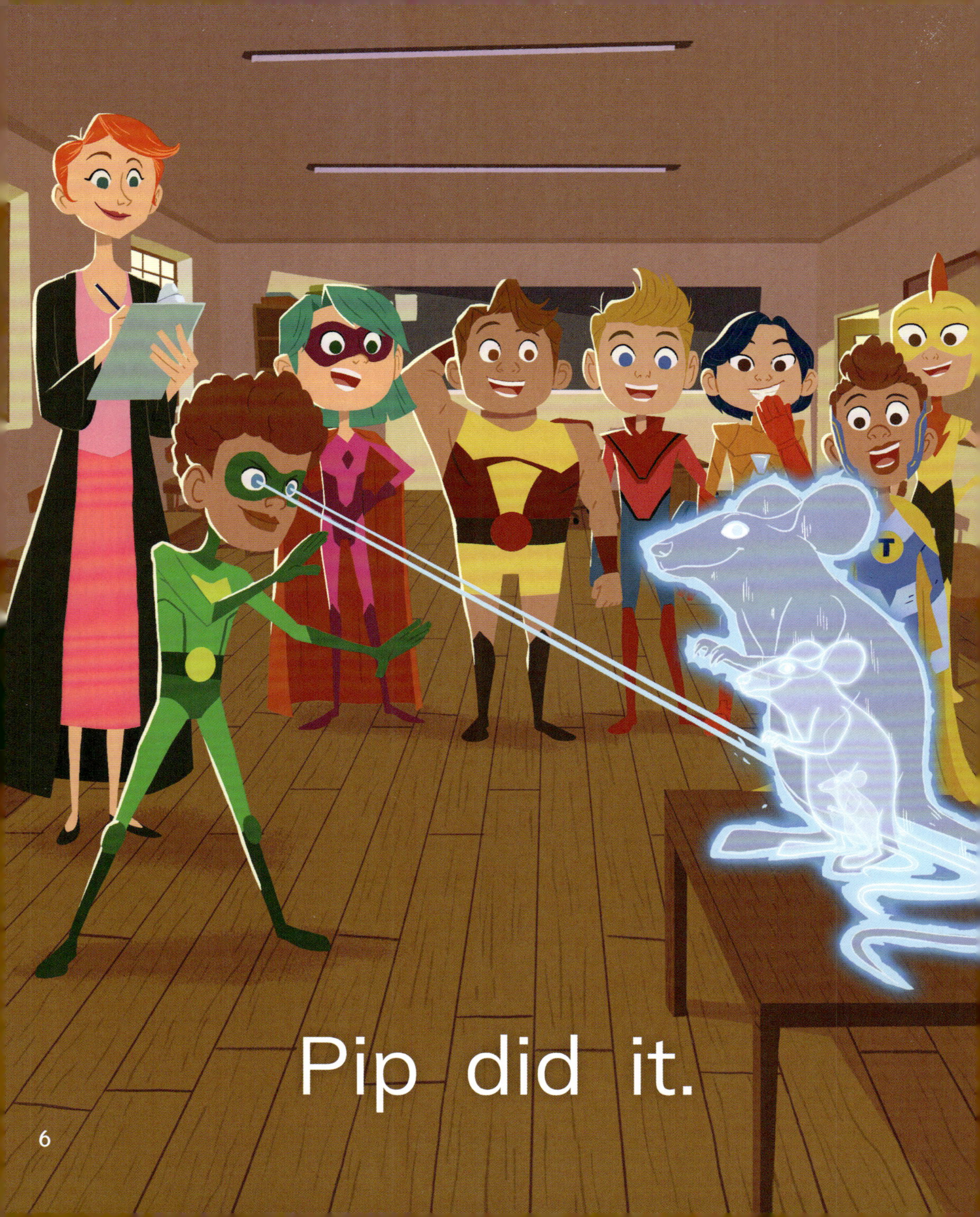

Pip did it.

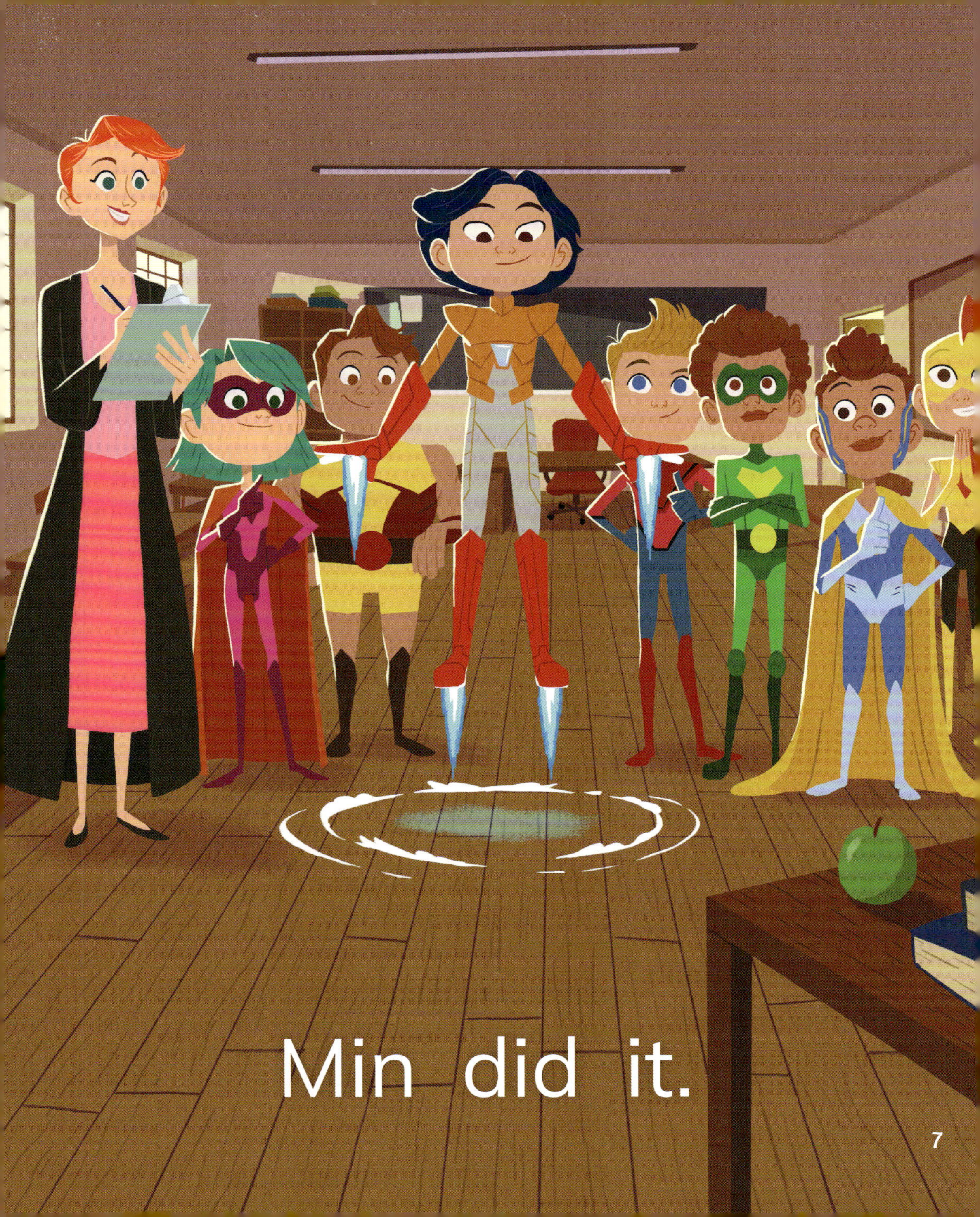

Min did it.

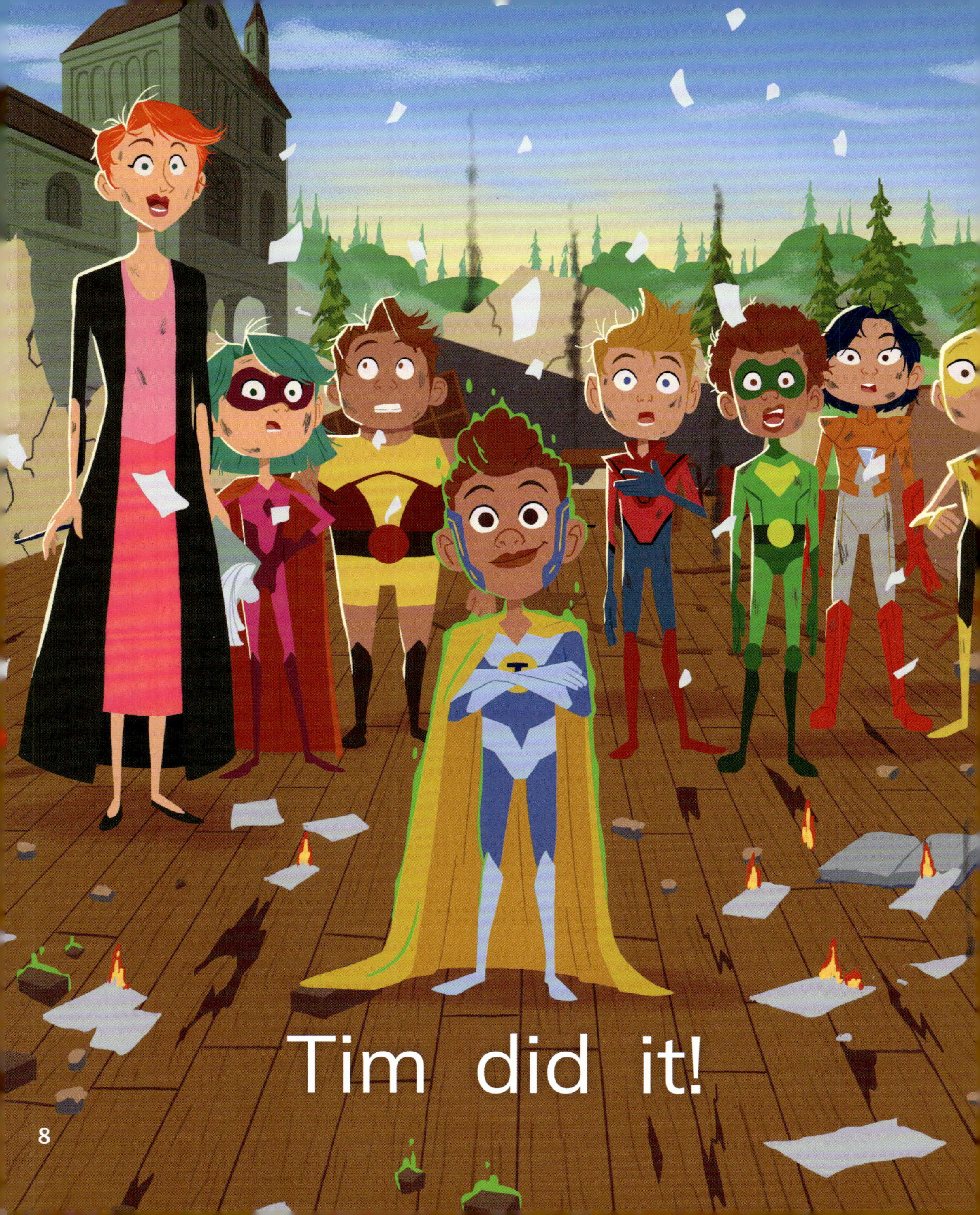

Tim did it!